ICH HALTE MEIN ZIMMER GERN SAUBER

I LOVE TO KEEP MY ROOM CLEAN

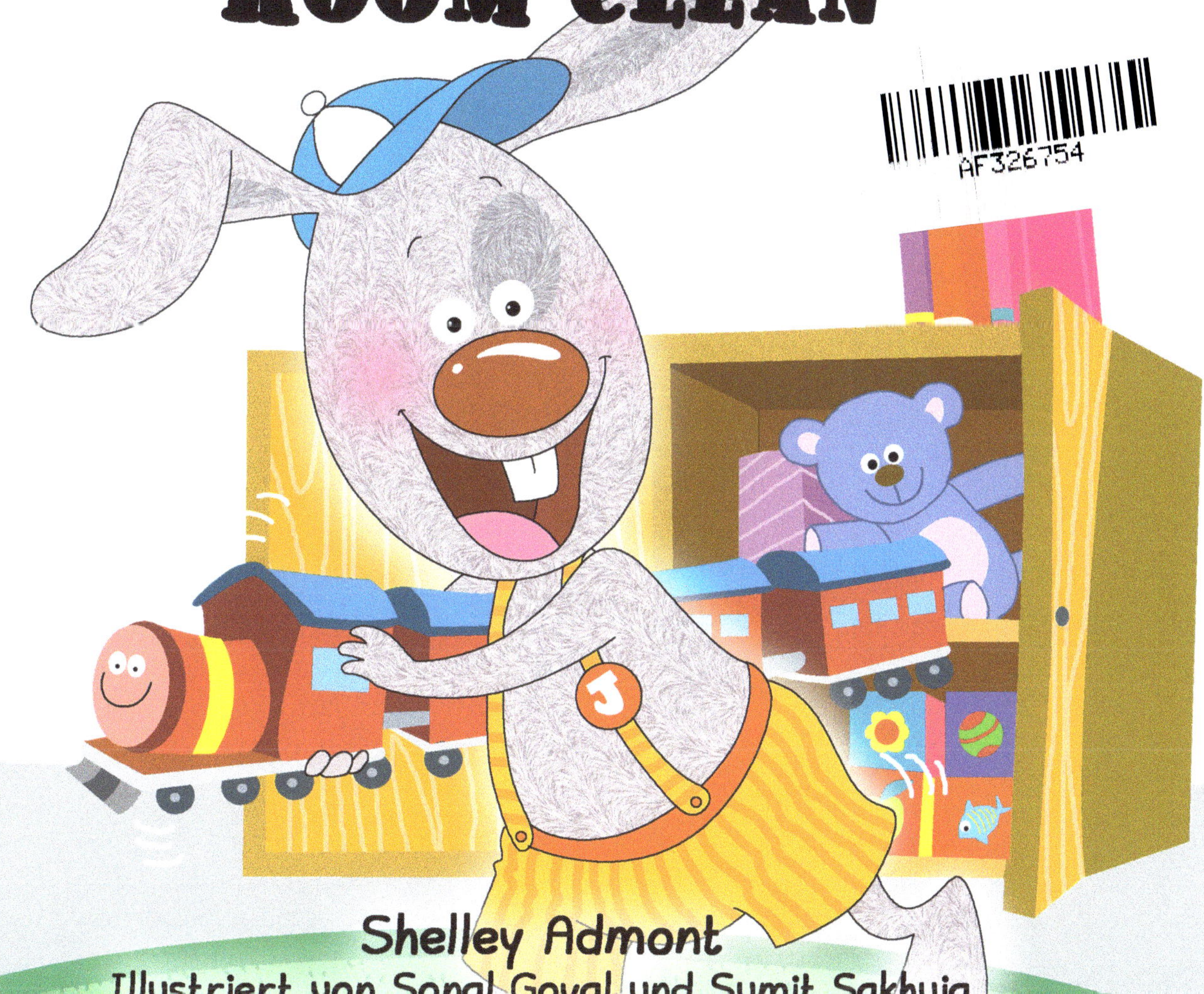

Shelley Admont

Illustriert von Sonal Goyal und Sumit Sakhuja

Translated from English by Tess Parthum
Aus dem Englischen übersetzt von Tess Parthum
German editing by Liane Meyer
Überarbeitung im Deutschen von Liane Meyer

Library and Archives Canada Cataloguing in Publication Data
I love to Keep My Room Clean (German English Bilingual Edition)/ Shelley Admont
ISBN: 978-1-77268-210-6 paperback
ISBN: 978-1-77268-595-4 hardcover
ISBN: 978-1-77268-209-0 ebook

Please note that the German and English versions of the story have been written to be as close as possible. However, in some cases they differ in order to accommodate nuances and fluidity of each language.

Für die, die ich am meisten liebe-S.A.

For those I love the most-S. A.

Es war ein sonniger Samstagmorgen in einem weit entfernten Wald. Drei Hasenbrüder waren soeben aufgewacht, als ihre Mama das Zimmer betrat.

It was a sunny Saturday morning in a faraway forest. Three bunny brothers had just woken up when their Mom entered the room.

„Guten Morgen, Jungs", sagte Mama. „Ich habe euch hier drinnen gehört."

"Good morning, boys," Mom said. "I heard you moving around in here."

„Heute ist Samstag, wir können so lange schlafen, wie wir wollen", sagte der mittlere Bruder mit einem Lächeln.

"Today is Saturday, we can sleep as late as we want," said the middle brother with a smile.

„Ihr könnt noch eine Weile in euren Betten bleiben", sagte Mama. „Aber ich muss bald los. Ich muss heute eure Oma besuchen, und ihr bleibt mit Papi hier, bis ich wiederkomme."

"You can stay in your beds for a while," Mom said, "but I'll have to leave. I need to visit your Granny today and you'll stay with Daddy until I come back."

„Wenn ihr aufgestanden seid und eure Zähne geputzt habt, werdet ihr frühstücken", fügte Mama hinzu. „Danach könnt ihr Bücher lesen oder mit euren Spielsachen spielen. Oder ihr könnt nach draußen gehen und mit euren Fahrrädern fahren."

"When you get out of your beds and brush your teeth, you'll have your breakfast," Mom added. "After that, you can read books or play with your toys. Or, you can go outside and ride your bicycles."

„Hurra!" Die Hasenbrüder fingen an, glücklich auf ihren Betten zu springen.

"Hooray!" The bunny brothers started to jump on their beds happily.

„Aber...", fuhr Mama fort, „ihr seid dafür verantwortlich, euer Zimmer sauberzumachen."

"But..." continued Mom, "you are responsible for cleaning your room."

„Wenn ich zurückkomme, möchte ich dieses Haus sauber und ordentlich vorfinden. Schafft ihr das?"
"When I come back, I want to see this house clean and organized, exactly as it is now. Can you do this?"

„Sicher, Mama", antwortete der älteste Bruder stolz. „Wir sind groß genug und wir können Verantwortung übernehmen."

"Sure, Mom," answered the oldest brother proudly. "We are big enough and we can be responsible."

Nachdem sie ihre Zähne geputzt hatten, servierte Papa ein leckeres Frühstück und ein noch köstlicheres Dessert. Dann fing der Spaß an!

After they brushed their teeth, Dad served a delicious breakfast and an even more delicious dessert. Then the fun began!

Die Häschen begannen damit, ihr Puzzle zusammenzusetzen. Dann machten sie mit ihren Holzbausteinen weiter. Danach spielten sie mit ihrer Eisenbahn.

The bunnies started by putting together their puzzle. Then they continued with their wooden building blocks. Next they turned on the train set and played together with the tracks.

„Diesen Zug mag ich am liebsten", sagte Jimmy, der jüngste Bruder, als er den An-Schalter umlegte.

"This railway train is my favorite," said Jimmy, the youngest brother, as he flipped the on switch.

„Das ist das beste Geschenk, das ich zu meinem letzten Geburtstag bekommen habe."

"This is the best present I've got on my last birthday."

Nachdem sie stundenlang drinnen gespielt hatten, fingen die Hasen langsam an, sich zu langweilen.

After playing inside for hours, the bunnies grew bored.

„Lasst uns draußen spielen gehen!", sagte der mittlere Bruder und sah aus dem Fenster.

"Let's go play outside!" said the middle brother, looking out the window.

„Ja! Aber wir müssen hier erst aufräumen", sagte der älteste Bruder.

"Yeah! But we need to clean up here first," said the oldest brother.

„Oh, wir haben noch genügend Zeit, bevor Mama zurückkommt", antwortete Jimmy. „Wir können später aufräumen." Die älteren Brüder stimmten zu, und sie gingen alle hinaus.

"Oh, we have enough time before Mom comes back," answered Jimmy, "we can clean up later." The older brothers agreed and they all went out.

Outside, the three bunny brothers enjoyed the sunny weather. They rode their bicycles and played hide and seek. Finally, they decided to play basketball.

"We'll need our basketball," said the oldest brother. "But I don't remember where we put it."

"I think it's under my bed," said Jimmy. "I'll go check." With that, he ran inside the house, hoping to find the ball.

Als er die Tür zu ihrem Zimmer öffnete, war er sehr überrascht. Der Boden war bedeckt mit Puzzleteilen, Bausteinen, Autos, Eisenbahnschienen und anderen Spielsachen.

When he opened the door to their room, he was very surprised. The floor was covered with puzzle pieces, building blocks, cars, tracks, and other toys.

Da liegen zu viele Sachen auf dem Boden herum, dachte Jimmy, als er zu seinem Bett ging.

There are too many things thrown on the floor, thought Jimmy, making his way toward his bed.

Letztendlich stolperte er und verlor das Gleichgewicht. Er versuchte, sich aufrecht zu halten, doch stattdessen fiel er genau auf seinen Lieblingszug.

Eventually, he stumbled and lost his balance. He was trying to stay upright, but instead fell directly on his favorite train.

„Autsch!", schrie er und sah zu, wie die Räder des Zuges in unterschiedliche Richtungen flogen. „Neeein, mein Zug!" Jimmy brach in Tränen aus.

"Ouch!" he screamed, watching the train's wheels flying in different directions. "Noooo, my train!" Jimmy burst into tears.

„Bist du in Ordnung, Liebling?" Papa erschien in der Tür. Aufgrund des ganzen Chaos passte er nicht in das Zimmer.

"Are you alright, honey?" Dad appeared at the door. He couldn't fit inside the room due to all the mess.

„Mir geht es gut. Aber mein Zug...", weinte Jimmy und zeigte auf die kaputten Räder seines Zuges.

"I'm fine. But my train..." cried Jimmy, pointing to the train's broken wheels.

„Ich kann den Zug nicht einmal sehen", sagte Papa. „Und was genau ist in diesem Zimmer passiert?"

"I can't even see the train," said Dad. "And what exactly happened in this room?"

„Jimmy, warum brauchst du so lange?", riefen die Stimmen der anderen Brüder, als sie ins Haus rannten.

"Jimmy, why's it taking you so long?" The other brothers shouted as they ran into the house.

„Mein Zug ist kaputtgegangen!" Jimmy hörte nicht auf zu weinen.

"My train broke!" Jimmy couldn't stop crying.

„Weine nicht, Jimmy", sagte der älteste Bruder. „Wir werden uns etwas einfallen lassen. Papa?"

"Don't cry, Jimmy," said the oldest brother. "We'll think of something. Dad?"

„Vielleicht könnte ich ihn reparieren", sagte Papa. „Aber ihr müsst hier aufräumen. Bringt mir den Zug und die Räder, wenn ihr sie gefunden habt." Damit ging Papa aus dem Zimmer.

"Maybe I could fix it," said Dad. "But you need to clean up here. Bring me the train and the wheels after you find them." With that, Dad went out of the room.

„Wir müssen uns beeilen, bevor Mama zurückkommt", sagte der älteste Bruder.

"We need to hurry, before Mom comes back," said the oldest brother.

„Oh, Aufräumen ist langweilig", sagte Jimmy seufzend und sah sich im Zimmer um.

"Oh, cleaning up is boring," said Jimmy sighing and looking around the messy room.

„Dann lasst uns ein Aufräum-Spiel spielen", rief sein älterer Bruder.

"Let's play a cleaning up game then," exclaimed his oldest brother.

Jimmy war plötzlich aufgeregt. „Der Sturm kommt bald!", schrie er. „Wir müssen all den Spielsachen helfen, zurück in ihre Häuser zu gelangen."

Jimmy became excited. "The storm is coming soon!" he shouted. "We need to help all the toys get back to their houses."

„Wir sind Superhelden", rief der mittlere Bruder.
Er hob Spielsachen vom Boden auf und legte jedes
an seinen rechtmäßigen Platz.

"We're superheroes," yelled the middle brother.
He picked up toys from the floor and put each one
in its proper place.

Spielend und mit Freude schafften die Brüder Ordnung und machten alles sauber.

Playing and enjoying themselves, the brothers organized and cleaned everything.

„Sämtliche Räder sind hier", rief Jimmy und rannte mit dem kaputten Zug und seinen Rädern in seinen Händen zu seinem Vater.

"All wheels are here," exclaimed Jimmy, running to his father with the broken train and its wheels in his hands.

„Hier, ich habe den Basketball gefunden!", schrie der mittlere Bruder aufgeregt.

"Here, I found the basketball!" screamed the middle brother with excitement.

„Leg ihn in seine Schachtel und... wir sind fertig", sagte der älteste Bruder glücklich.

"Put it in its box and... we are finished," said the oldest brother happily.

„Es hat wirklich Spaß gemacht", sagte der mittlere Bruder und setzte sich auf sein Bett. „Aber wir haben eine ganze Stunde gebraucht."

"It was really fun," said the middle brother, sitting down on his bed. "But it took us a whole hour."

„Nein!“, schrie Jimmy, als er ins Zimmer kam.
„Setz dich nicht dorthin!“
"No!" yelled Jimmy as he entered the room.
"Don't sit there!"

„Was? Warum?!“, fragte der mittlere Bruder und
sprang vom Bett.
"What? Why?!" asked the middle brother, jumping
off the bed.

„Du hast gerade dein Bett gemacht. Wenn du dich
jetzt daraufsetzt, musst du es nochmal machen“,
erklärte Jimmy.
"You just made your bed. If you sit on it now,
you'd have to make it again," explained Jimmy.

„Vielleicht könnten wir jetzt ein Buch lesen“,
schlug der ältere Bruder vor und ging zum
Bücherregal.
"Maybe we could read a book now," suggested the
oldest brother, approaching the bookshelf.

„Fass diese Bücher nicht an“, rief Jimmy. „Ich
habe sie alle nach Farben sortiert!“
"Don't touch those books," shouted Jimmy."I
organized them all by color!“

„Tut mir leid", sagte der älteste Bruder. „Aber was werden wir machen? Wir dürfen mit nichts spielen."
"Sorry," said the oldest brother. "But what will we do? We can't play with anything."

They thought for a while and then the oldest brother shouted: "I have an idea!"

"What if we clean up after each game?" he suggested. "Then it won't take so much time to put toys away."

"Let's try," said Jimmy happily.

First, the oldest brother read a beautiful book to his younger brothers. When they finished reading, he put it back on the shelf.

Als Nächstes bauten sie aus ihren bunten Bausteinen einen großen Turm. Als sie fertig waren, legten sie die Bausteine zurück in die Kiste – und das Zimmer blieb ordentlich!

Next, they built a large tower out of their colorful blocks. When they were done, they put the blocks back into the box — and the room stayed clean!

In diesem Moment klopften Mama und Papa an die Tür.
At that moment, Mom and Dad knocked on the door.

„Ich habe euch so sehr vermisst", sagte Mama. „Aber ich sehe, dass ihr es geschafft habt, euer Zimmer sauber zu halten. Ich bin so stolz auf euch."
"I missed you so much," said Mom, "but I see you managed to keep your room clean. I'm so proud of you."

„Und hier ist dein Zug, Jimmy", sagte Papa und gab ihm das Spielzeug. Die Räder waren repariert und Jimmy lächelte strahlend.
"And here's your train, Jimmy," said Dad, handing him the toy. The wheels were fixed and Jimmy smiled widely.

„Wer möchte die Kekse probieren, die Oma für uns gemacht hat?", fragte Mama.
"Who wants to try cookies that Granny made for you?" asked Mom.

„*Ich!*", riefen die Hasenbrüder und ihr Papa.

"Me!" shouted the bunny brothers and their Dad.

„*Aber wir werden sie in der Küche essen, nicht in diesem sauberen Zimmer*", sagte Jimmy sehr ernst. „*Stimmt's, Mama?*"

"But we'll eat them in the kitchen, not in this clean room," said Jimmy very seriously. "Right, Mom?"

Die ganze Familie fing laut an zu lachen. Sie gingen in die Küche, um Kekse zu essen.

The whole family started laughing loudly. They went to the kitchen to eat cookies.

Von diesem Tag an hielten die Brüder ihr Zimmer gern sauber und ordentlich. Sie spielten mit all ihren Spielsachen, aber wenn sie fertig waren, legten sie alle zurück an ihren Platz.

Since that day, the brothers loved to keep their room clean and organized. They played with all their toys, but when they finished, they put everything back in its place.

Sie brauchten nie wieder lange, um ihr Zimmer aufzuräumen.

It never took them long to clean up their room again.